THE MAGIC BUS
LOST IN THE SOLAR SYSTEM

By Joanna Cole   **Illustrated by Bruce Degen**

Kingfisher Books

The author and illustrator wish to thank
Dr Donna L. Gresh, Centre for Radar Astronomy
at Stanford University, for her assistance
in preparing this book.

The author also thanks John Stoke,
Astronomical Writer/Producer
at the American Museum-Hayden Planetarium,
for his helpful advice.

Kingfisher Books, Grisewood & Dempsey Ltd,
Elsley House, 24–30 Great Titchfield Street,
London W1P 7AD

First published in paperback in the UK in 1992 by Kingfisher Books
10 9 8 7 6 5 4 3 2
First published in hardback in the UK in 1991 by Kingfisher Books
Published by arrangement with Scholastic Inc.

Text copyright © 1990 by Joanna Cole
Illustrations copyright © 1990 by Bruce Degen

BRITISH LIBRARY CATALOGUING-IN-PUBLICATION DATA
A catalogue record for this book is available
from the British Library

ISBN 0 86272 867 3

Printed in Spain

To Virginia and Bob McBride J.C.

For Chris, queen of the
Biscadorian Mother ship B.D.

WHAT IS THE
SOLAR SYSTEM?
by John

The solar system is the Sun and all the bodies that orbit around it — the nine planets, their moons, the asteroids (chunks of rock) and comets (balls of ice and dust).

It was field trip day again for Ms Frizzle's class. Everyone was excited. We were going to the planetarium to see a sky show about the solar system.

CLASS, AN ORBIT IS THE PATH OF A PLANET OR OTHER OBJECT AROUND THE SUN.

SUN

ORBIT

AL·EINSTEIN
E = mc²
MY FAVOURITE THEORIST

ALFALFA
MY FAVOURITE SPROUT

We tried to be nice to Janet.
We really did.
As we got on the school bus,
we told her that Ms Frizzle
is the weirdest teacher in school.
But Janet wasn't interested.
She wanted to tell us about herself.

As usual, it took a while to get the old bus started. But finally we were on our way. As we were driving, Ms Frizzle told us all about how the Earth spins like a top as it moves in its orbit. It was just a short drive to the planetarium, but Ms Frizzle talked fast.

THIS BUS IS A WRECK.

AT LEAST IT STARTED THIS TIME.

WE HAVE NEW SCHOOL BUSES AT OUR SCHOOL.

WHAT MAKES NIGHT AND DAY?
by Phoebe

The spinning of the Earth makes night and day.
When one side of the Earth faces the Sun it is daytime on that side. When that side turns away from the Sun, it is night.

WHEN THE EARTH SPINS WE SAY IT ROTATES. THE EARTH MAKES ONE COMPLETE ROTATION— TURN—EVERY 24 HOURS.

When we got to the planetarium,
it was closed for repairs.
"Class, this means we'll
have to return to school,"
said the Friz.
We were so disappointed!

On the way back,
as we were waiting at a red light,
something amazing happened.
The bus started tilting back,
and we heard the roar of rockets.
"Oh, dear," said Ms Frizzle.
"We seem to be blasting off!"

Far behind, in the black sky,
we saw the planet Earth
getting smaller and smaller.
We were travelling in space!
We had become astronauts!

The Friz said our first stop
would be the Moon.
We got off the bus and looked around.
There was no air, no water,
no sign of life.
All we saw were dust and rock
and lots and lots of craters.
Ms Frizzle said the craters were
formed millions of years ago
when the Moon was hit by meteorites.
Meteorites are falling chunks
of rock and metal.

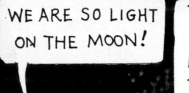

WE ARE SO LIGHT ON THE MOON!

THAT'S BECAUSE THE MOON HAS LESS GRAVITY THAN THE EARTH.

YOUR WEIGHT AND RATE ON THE MOON

Kg.	Kg.
39	7
Earth Weight	Moon Weight

You will travel to far off places.

It was fun on the Moon.
We wanted to play,
but Ms Frizzle said it was time to go.
So we got back on the bus.
"We'll start with the Sun,
the centre of the solar system,"
said the Friz, and we blasted off.

LOOK HOW HIGH WE CAN JUMP!

I WAS IN A NATIONAL SKIPPING CONTEST. I WON, OF COURSE.

IS THERE A NATIONAL BRAGGING CONTEST?

WHAT MAKES THE MOON SHINE?
by Rachel
The Moon does not make any light of its own. The moonlight we see from Earth is really light from the sun. It hits the Moon and bounces off, the way light is reflected from a mirror.

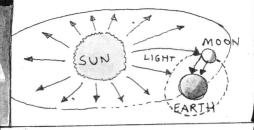

THE MOON'S ORBIT
by Amanda Jane
The Moon travels in orbit around the Earth, just as the Earth travels around the Sun.

THE SUN IS A STAR
by Carmen
Our Sun is an average star like the ones we see in the night sky.

WHICH STAR DO WE SEE ONLY IN THE DAYTIME?

THAT'S EASY: THE SUN.

HOW BIG IS THE SUN?
by Gregory
Our sun measures more than a million kilometres across. More than one million Earths could fit inside it!

We zoomed towards the Sun, the biggest, brightest, and hottest object in the solar system. Jets of super-hot gases shot out at us from the surface. Thank goodness Ms Frizzle didn't get *too* close!

YOU SHOULD NEVER LOOK DIRECTLY AT THE SUN, CHILDREN. IT CAN DAMAGE YOUR EYES!

YOU SHOULD NEVER DRIVE A BUS DIRECTLY INTO THE SUN, EITHER!

HOT!

SOLAR FLARES are giant storms on the Sun's surface.

She steered around to the other side
and pulled away.
"We'll be seeing all the planets
in order, class," explained Frizzie.
"Mercury is the first planet,
the closest to the Sun."

MY SCHOOL IS HEATED
WITH <u>SOLAR</u> ENERGY.

I HAVE A <u>SUN</u> DECK.

I HAVE TEN PAIRS
OF <u>SUN</u>GLASSES.

GIVE US A
BREAK, JANET.

HOW HOT IS THE SUN?
by Florrie
At the centre of
the sun the temper-
ature is about
15 <u>million</u> degrees
Centigrade! The sun
is so hot it heats
planets that are
millions of kilometres
away.

SUN SPOTS
are areas
that are cooler
than the rest
of the Sun.

Our Path So Far

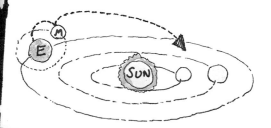

Mercury was a dead, sun-baked planet.
"This planet is a lot like our Moon.
There is no water and hardly any air,"
said the Friz.
"Notice the craters on its surface
as we pass by."

THE SUN LOOKS TWICE AS BIG HERE AS IT DOES FROM EARTH.

THAT'S BECAUSE MERCURY IS SO CLOSE.

TOO CLOSE! LET'S GO!

YOUR WEIGHT AND FATE ON MERCURY

Kg.	Kg.
39	15
Earth Weight	Mercury Weight

You will holiday in a sunny spot.

Before long, we felt ourselves
being pulled in by the gravity of Venus
– the second planet from the Sun.
Venus was completely covered by
a thick layer of yellowish clouds.
"We will now explore the surface of Venus,"
said Ms Frizzle.

WHY ARE VENUS'S CLOUDS YELLOW?
by Tim
Earth's clouds are white because they are made of water vapour.
Venus's clouds are made mostly of a deadly yellow poison called sulphuric acid.

WE'RE GAINING WEIGHT, AND WE HAVEN'T EVEN HAD LUNCH.

WE WILL BE HEAVIER HERE THAN ON THE MOON OR MERCURY BECAUSE VENUS HAS MORE GRAVITY.

YOUR WEIGHT AND FATE ON VENUS

Kg. 39 Earth Weight
Kg. 35 Venus weight

Your future looks Cloudy.

SO DOES VENUS!

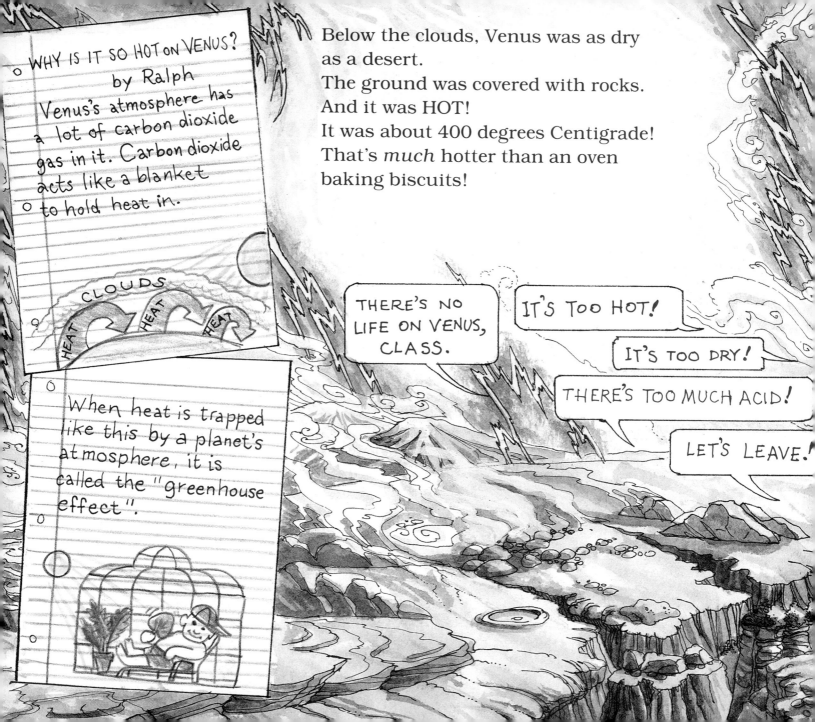

WHY IS IT SO HOT ON VENUS?
by Ralph
Venus's atmosphere has a lot of carbon dioxide gas in it. Carbon dioxide acts like a blanket to hold heat in.

CLOUDS
HEAT HEAT HEAT

When heat is trapped like this by a planet's atmosphere, it is called the "greenhouse effect".

Below the clouds, Venus was as dry as a desert.
The ground was covered with rocks.
And it was HOT!
It was about 400 degrees Centigrade!
That's *much* hotter than an oven baking biscuits!

THERE'S NO LIFE ON VENUS, CLASS.

IT'S TOO HOT!

IT'S TOO DRY!

THERE'S TOO MUCH ACID!

LET'S LEAVE!

The air was so heavy
we could feel it pressing down on us!
Ms Frizzle said there might be volcanoes
around, too.
We said, "Let's get out of here!"
"Our next stop is Mars,
the red planet, fourth from the Sun,"
announced the Friz.
"On our way, we'll be passing through
the orbit of Earth, the third planet."
The bus lifted off with a roar.

I'VE BEEN TO MARS
LOTS OF TIMES.

JUST
IGNORE HER.

IT NEVER RAINS
ON VENUS
by Dorothy Ann
Venus's clouds
never make rain
because it is too hot
for rain to form. Any
liquid on Venus dries
up instantly.

Our Path So Far

Looking down, we saw a huge canyon.
Ms Frizzle said it would stretch from
London to New York, if it were on Earth.
There was a volcano
more than twice as high
as the highest volcano on Earth.
And all around, there were channels
that looked like dried-up river beds.

IS THERE LIFE ON MARS?
by Molly
No life has been found on Mars. Living things need water, and there is no liquid water on Mars.
So space scientists think life probably cannot exist there!

Polar Ice Cap

Canyon

Channels

YOUR WEIGHT AND FATE ON MARS

kg. 39 Earth Weight	kg. 15 Mars Weight

EARTH IS THE BEST PLANET FOR LIFE. THAT'S WHY I LIVE THERE.

Things will look rosy soon.

JANET LIKES TO BE THE BEST.

WE NOTICED.

"Mars is the last of what we call
the inner planets!"
Ms Frizzle shouted above the roar of the rockets.
"We will now be going
through the asteroid belt
to the outer planets!"

WHAT ARE THE
INNER PLANETS?
by Alex
The inner planets
are the four planets
closest to the sun—
Mercury, Venus,
Earth and Mars.
The four inner
planets are all
hard and rocky.

THE ASTEROID BELT
by Shirley

The area between the inner and the outer planets is called the asteroid belt. It is filled with thousands and thousands of asteroids.

WHAT ARE ASTEROIDS?
by Florrie

Asteroids are chunks of rock and metal in orbit around the Sun.

Scientists think they are the building blocks of a planet that never formed.

Thousands of asteroids were spinning all around us.
All at once, we heard the tinkling of broken glass.
One of our tail-lights had been hit by an asteroid.
Ms Frizzle put the bus on autopilot and went out to take a look.
She kept on talking about asteroids over the bus radio.

THE LARGEST ASTEROID IS ONLY ⅓ THE SIZE OF OUR MOON. MOST ASTEROIDS ARE THE SIZE OF HOUSES OR SMALLER.

I WISH SHE'D COME INSIDE.

Suddenly there was a snap.
Ms Frizzle's tether line had broken!
Without warning,
the rockets fired up,
and the bus zoomed away!
The autopilot was malfunctioning.

On the radio, Ms Frizzle's voice grew fainter and fainter.
Then she was gone.
We were on our own!
We were lost in the solar system!

Most of us were too scared to move.
But Janet started searching the bus.
In the glove compartment
she found Ms Frizzle's lesson book.
As she began reading from it,
a huge planet came into view.
"Class, this is Jupiter," Janet read.
"It's the first of the outer planets,
and the largest planet in the solar system."

"As we approach Jupiter, we can see some of its 16 moons."

"Arnold, are you listening?"

BOY, Ms FRIZZLE PLANS EVERYTHING!

SHE SHOULDN'T TOUCH Ms FRIZZLE'S THINGS.

BUT THIS IS AN EMERGENCY!

Lesson Plan
As we approach
Jupiter, we can
see some of its
16 moons.
"Arnold, are
...?"

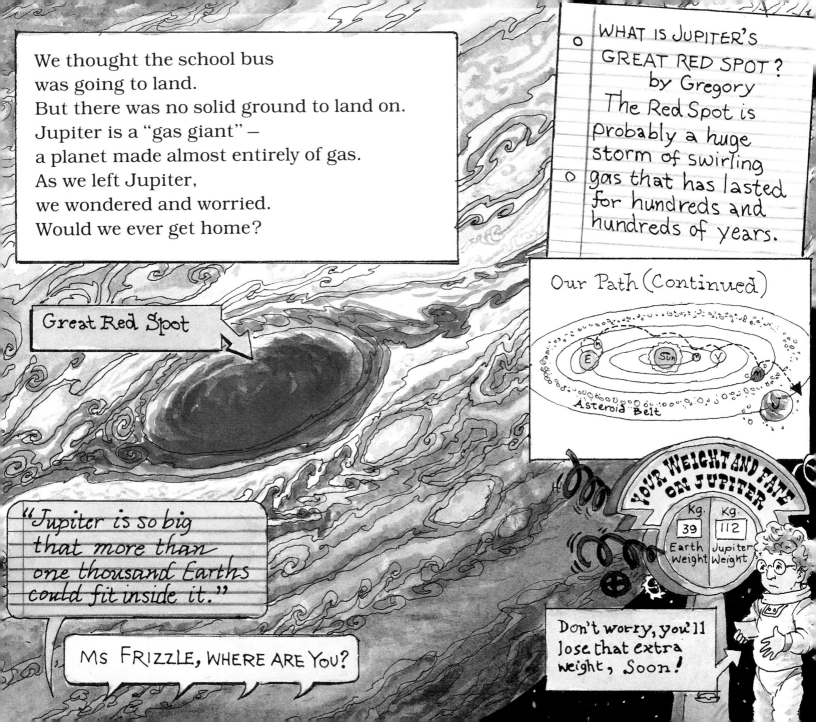

We thought the school bus
was going to land.
But there was no solid ground to land on.
Jupiter is a "gas giant" –
a planet made almost entirely of gas.
As we left Jupiter,
we wondered and worried.
Would we ever get home?

WHAT IS JUPITER'S GREAT RED SPOT?
by Gregory
The Red Spot is probably a huge storm of swirling gas that has lasted for hundreds and hundreds of years.

Our Path (Continued)

Asteroid Belt

Great Red Spot

"Jupiter is so big that more than one thousand Earths could fit inside it."

MS FRIZZLE, WHERE ARE YOU?

YOUR WEIGHT AND FATE ON JUPITER

Kg. 39 Earth Weight

Kg. 112 Jupiter Weight

Don't worry, you'll lose that extra weight, soon!

The next sight made us forget our troubles.
It was Saturn, a gas planet like Jupiter.
It had swirling clouds and lots of moons.
But the most incredible thing about Saturn
was its rings.
It was the most beautiful planet
in the solar system!

WHAT ARE SATURN'S RINGS?
by Rachel
Saturn's rings are made of ice, rock and dust—all in orbit around the planet.

YOUR WEIGHT AND FATE ON SATURN

Kg.	Kg.
39	41
Earth Weight	Saturn Weight

There's a ring in your future.

"There are thousands of rings around Saturn, class."

THEY LOOK LIKE THE GROOVES IN A RECORD.

SATURN IS THE GROOVIEST PLANET, MAN!

The bus was going faster and faster,
and we couldn't control the autopilot.
We swept past stormy Neptune,
another blue-green planet – eighth from the Sun.
All we could think about
was finding Ms Frizzle!

HOW LONG IS A YEAR?
by Tim
A year is the time it takes for a planet to go all around the sun. Neptune and Uranus are so far away from the sun that they have very long years.

One year on Uranus is 84 Earth years.

Neptune's year is 165 Earth years.

"Neptune is the last of the giant gas planets."

WE'RE ALMOST OUT OF GAS OURSELVES!

Great Dark Spot

AND THE NEAREST SERVICE STATION IS 4,000 MILLION KILOMETRES AWAY.

YOUR WEIGHT AND FATE ON NEPTUNE

Kg. 39 Earth Weight

Kg 44 Neptune Weight

You will have a happy birthday 165 years from now.

IS PLUTO A REAL PLANET?
by Wanda
Some scientists think Pluto was once a moon of Neptune. It may have escaped from the orbit around Neptune. Then it became a real planet in orbit around the Sun. Pluto was the last planet discovered in the known solar system.

YOUR WEIGHT AND FATE ON PLUTO

Kg. 39 Earth Weight	Kg. 0.5 Pluto Weight

You will meet a small, dark planet.

CHARON

PLUTO

We were going so fast,
we almost missed seeing the ninth planet,
tiny Pluto,* and its moon, Charon.
We were so far away from the Sun that it
didn't look big any more.
It just looked like a very bright star.
We were leaving the solar system.

*Every 248 years, Neptune's orbit is further out than Pluto's. Then Neptune is the ninth planet. But most of the time, Pluto is the ninth planet from the Sun.

THERE'S NOTHING OUT THERE — BUT STARS.

MAYBE THERE'S A TENTH PLANET WAITING TO BE DISCOVERED.

IT'LL HAVE TO WAIT.

I HOPE MS FRIZZLE IS WAITING, TOO.

Janet flipped rapidly
through Ms Frizzle's book.
Suddenly she found something new –
the instructions for the autopilot.
We punched in ASTEROID BELT
on the control panel.
Slowly the bus turned around.
It was working! We were going back!

ASTEROID BELT **

Auto-Pilot

JANET REALLY SAVED THE DAY.

I TOLD YOU SHE'S A GOOD KID.

BEYOND PLUTO:
STARS AND MORE STARS
by Alex
Beyond our solar system are millions and millions of stars. There are so many stars and they are so far away that our minds cannot even imagine it.
Some of those stars may have planets, and some of those

planets could have life on them, just like our earth.

Our Path so far

E M S M V M J S
Asteroid Belt
U N P

With Frizzie back at the wheel,
the bus headed straight for Earth.
We re-entered the atmosphere,
landed with a thump,
and looked around.

We were in the school car park again.
The rockets were gone.
The space suits were gone.
The bus was a wreck.
Everything was back to normal.

OUR PLANET CHART

PLANET	HOW BIG ACROSS	HOW LONG ONE ROTATION (DAY AND NIGHT)	HOW LONG ONE YEAR	HOW FAR FROM THE SUN	HOW MANY MOONS	HOW MANY RINGS
MERCURY	4,850 km.	59 days	88 days	58 million km.	None	None
VENUS	12,140 km.	244 days	224 days	108 million km.	None	None
EARTH	12,756 km.	23.56 hours	365.25 days	150 million km.	1	None
MARS	6,790 km.	24.37 hours	687 days	228 million km.	2	None
JUPITER	142,600 km.	9.50 hours	11.9 Earth years	778 million km.	at least 16	2
SATURN	120,200 km.	10.14 hours	29.5 Earth years	1,427 million km.	at least 17	Many
URANUS	49,000 km.	11 hours	84 Earth years	2,870 million km.	at least 15	10
NEPTUNE	50,000 km	15.48 hours	164.8 Earth years	4,497 million km.	8	4
PLUTO	about 3,000 km.	153 hours	247.7 Earth years	5,900 million km.	1	None

In the classroom, we made a terrific chart of the planets and a mobile of the solar system.

OUR SOLAR SYSTEM

Sun

⑥Saturn

Neptune

Asteroid Belt

③Earth

①Mercury

②Venus

④Mars

⑤Jupiter

⑦Uranus

⑨Pluto

YOUR WEIGHT AND FATE ON EARTH

Kg.
39
Earth Weight

HOW ABOUT THAT? I WEIGH 39 KILOGRAMS.

There's no place like home.

At last, it was time to go home.
It had been a typical day
in Ms Frizzle's class.
Now we had only one problem.
Would anyone ever believe us
when we told about our trip?

ATTENTION, READERS!

DO NOT ATTEMPT THIS TRIP ON YOUR OWN SCHOOL BUS!

Three reasons why not:

1. Attaching rockets to the school bus will upset your teacher, the school head teacher, and your parents. It will not get you into orbit anyway. An ordinary bus cannot travel in outer space, and you cannot become astronauts without years of training.

2. Landing on certain planets may be dangerous to your health. Even astronauts cannot visit Venus (it's too hot), Mercury (it's too close to the Sun), or Jupiter (its gravity would crush human beings). People cannot fly to the Sun, either. Its gravity and heat would be too strong.

3. Space travel could make you miss tea with your family . . . for the rest of your childhood. Even if a school bus *could* go to outer space, it could never travel through the entire solar system in one day. It took *years* for the Voyager space probes to do that.

ON THE OTHER HAND . . .

If a red-haired teacher in a funny dress shows up at your school – start packing!